Chinese Australians

Book 4

The Chinese Experience

The Untold Story of Prejudice and Violence on the Australian Goldfields

Marji Hill

Published by The Prison Tree Press 2025

Copyright © 2025 Marji Hill

The Prison Tree Press
Suite 124
1-10 Albert Avenue
Broadbeach, Queensland 4218
https://marjihill.com

ISBN: 9781763738485 Hardback
ISBN: 9781763738492 eBook

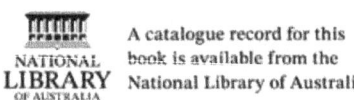 A catalogue record for this book is available from the National Library of Australia

All rights reserved. No part of this book may be reproduced, stored in a retrieval system, or transmitted in any form or by any means, electronic, mechanical, photocopying, recording, scanning, or otherwise, without the prior written permission of the publisher.

Disclaimer:

All the material contained in this book is provided for educational and informational purposes only. No responsibility can be taken for any results or outcomes resulting from the use of this material.

While every care has been taken to trace and acknowledge copyright the publishers tender their apologies for any accidental infringement where copyright has proved untraceable.

Every attempt has been made to provide information that is both accurate and effective, however, the author does not assume any responsibility for the accuracy or use/misuse of this information.

Acknowledgement is given to Canva for most of the illustrations in this book. The paintings, however, were created by Marji Hill.

THE SERIES

Chinese Australians

Book 1

Australia and China

Before Captain Cook

Book 2

Early Chinese Migrants

The First Chinese Australians

Book 3

Chinese and Gold

The Chinese on the Australian Goldfields

Book 4

The Chinese Experience

The Untold Story of Prejudice and Violence on the Australian Goldfields

Book 5

The Chinese Legacy

How Migration, Culture and Community have Influenced Australia

Acknowledgements

I acknowledge the Traditional Custodians
of Country throughout Australia
and their connections to land, sea, and community.

I pay my respect to elders, past, present, and emerging
and extend my respect to all First Nations peoples today.
In the spirit of reconciliation,
my mission is to increase understanding
between the First Nations and other Australians
and to provide people from all over the globe
some basic understanding of Australia's first people,
their history, and cultures.

In addition,
I thank Eddie Dowd for helping me get this book
into its final form for publication.
I also acknowledge the support
from John and Sherien Foley.

Marji Hill

Table of Contents

1.	Not Everyone Was Welcoming	1
2.	Why This Anti-Chinese Sentiment	3
3.	Laws Against the Chinese	5
4.	The Buckland Valley Riot	7
5.	From Tension to Violence	9
6.	What Happened to the Rioters?	11
7.	Lambing Flat	13
8.	The Chinese were different	15
9.	The "Roll-Up" Banner	17
10.	The Lambing Flat Riot	19
11.	The Aftermath	21
12.	What Can We Learn?	23

GLOSSARY	25
SOURCES	27
ABOUT MARJI HILL	29
MORE BOOKS BY MARJI HILL	31

1. Not Everyone Was Welcoming

When gold was discovered in Australia in the 1850s, people came rushing from all over the world to try their luck. But not everyone welcomed the Chinese.

Gold mine

From around 1850 onwards, anti-Chinese feelings grew. This negativity was caused by many things. There was competition over finding gold and misunderstandings about Chinese culture. Many Europeans held the racist belief that some people were better than others simply because they looked different and the colour of their skin.

The Chinese followed their own customs

A belief at the time was white racial superiority. This led to the perception that Chinese immigrants were inferior and undesirable.

Unfortunately, these attitudes resulted in bullying, unfair laws, and violence.

2. Why This Anti-Chinese Sentiment

Some Europeans believed that the Chinese were a threat. This was especially true on the goldfields, where everyone was desperate to find gold. When gold became harder to find, people got even more protective and suspicious.

Everyone was desperate to find gold

But there was more to the anger than just money.

The Chinese looked different. They spoke a different language. They ate different foods and wore different clothes. Some had long pigtails, and their wide-brimmed straw hats and footwear stood out.

They also followed religions like Buddhism and Taoism, which many Europeans did not understand. Because of all these differences, some Europeans treated them unfairly or even spread rumours about them.

These differences together with false stories about the Chinese all helped to spread fear and hate, even though most Chinese miners were peaceful and were just trying to make a living.

3. Laws Against the Chinese

Because of these negative attitudes, some colonial governments like Victoria and New South Wales made laws to try to keep Chinese people out of Australia — or to make life harder for them once they arrived.

For example, they introduced a "poll tax" which meant Chinese people had to pay money just to enter the country. They also limited how many Chinese passengers could come on a ship. These rules were made to slow down Chinese immigration and stop more people from arriving.

All of these actions and attitudes eventually led to the White Australia Policy.

This policy was made official in 1901. It was designed to keep Australia mostly white by stopping people from Asia and other non-European countries from coming to live here.

The White Australia Policy stayed in place for many decades and was not removed until the Whitlam Government in 1973. That year was a milestone in the history of the Chinese in Australia. The Hon. A.J. Grassby, a high-profile Minister for Immigration in the Whitlam government, was best known for his role in the initiation of multiculturalism and the ending of the White Australia Policy.

4. The Buckland Valley Riot

One of the worst events during this time of anti-Chinese hatred happened in 1857, at a place called Buckland Valley in Victoria. It became known as the Buckland Valley Riot.

Buckland Valley

At the time, there were around 2,000 Chinese miners working in the area. Gold was becoming harder to find, and many European miners had left. The Chinese moved in and worked hard. They would rework claims that the Europeans had abandoned.

Their mining techniques were clever and successful at finding gold. This made some European miners very jealous. Instead of respecting the Chinese for their hard work, they began spreading nasty stories—accusing them of smoking opium, gambling and other behaviour they did not like.

These stories created even more hatred and suspicion.

5. From Tension to Violence

Tensions grew worse and worse. The Europeans at the time found themselves in the minority because so many Chinese had moved onto the goldfield.

Attitudes were hostile

Attitudes towards the Chinese were volatile and hostile. Anger flared. Anti-Chinese placards appeared calling for all Chinese to be driven off the goldfields.

The Europeans would claim-jump profitable Chinese mines. They aggressively attacked Chinese miners, beating them, stoning them and cutting off their pigtails.

If any Europeans were arrested and taken off to court for anti-Chinese behaviour, European juries returned verdicts of not guilty. Violence became common.

The worst of the violence happened on American Independence Day, on 4 July 1857. A group of men, many of them Americans, left a local hotel with axe handles and clubs. They joined with others who were ready to drive the Chinese out of the Buckland Valley.

They destroyed tents, robbed Chinese miners and incinerated their belongings. The Chinese temple — newly built — was set on fire and burned to the ground.

Some reports say that three Chinese men were killed but there were also rumours of a much larger massacre. It is believed that many others may have died or been injured as they fled.

6. What Happened to the Rioters?

After the riot, twelve Europeans were charged. But even though there were many witnesses, only three were given light punishments. The rest were found "not guilty".

At the time, courts and juries were made up of people who often shared the same racist attitudes.

The Buckland Valley Riot was a brutal example of how unfairly Chinese people were treated in Australia.

7. Lambing Flat

Just a few years later, another terrible event took place in New South Wales (NSW). This was in a town then known as Lambing Flat (now called Young). What happened at Lambing Flat in 1861 was a horrific explosion of racial violence.

But this was not an isolated expression of aggression against the Chinese in NSW. Anti-Chinese tensions had surfaced in many other NSW areas as well.

Gold had been discovered in the area in 1860 and miners came in their thousands.

But Chinese miners, those who had faced discrimination in Victoria, also made their way to Lambing Flat, hoping to find better luck.

They did not come alone.

Many Chinese miners travelled in groups, sometimes with up to 200 men, all recruited by businesses or merchants in Australia and China.

Most came under a system called "credit-ticket," where someone else paid for their travel, and the miners paid them back later using a share of the gold they found.

Once they arrived, the Chinese worked together, reworking old claims and building their own mining systems like dams and channels. They were very organised and often successful.

The gold mining cradle was used to mine alluvial gold

But their success made others angry.

8. The Chinese were different

The Chinese were different in many ways, and some people did not like it. Their clothes, their language, their food and their religion all seemed strange to the European miners. Jealousy, fear, and racism were mixed and this created a dangerous environment.

**The Chinese were different
in many ways**

Some Europeans accused the Chinese of wasting water or taking over old claims. They did not like their religion or like their style of mining. And, most notably, they did not like seeing them succeed.

Soon, small fights and arguments turned into organised hate.

The Chinese wore distinctive hats

9. The "Roll-Up" Banner

In late 1860, a group of angry European miners formed a committee and decided that the Chinese had to go. They made a banner that said, "Roll-up, Roll-up, No Chinese" and carried it at public meetings.

Roll Up Banner

This banner became a symbol of anti-Chinese racism and was one of the earliest protest banners in Australian history. It also reflected the dangerous beliefs that would later become part of the White Australia Policy.

The banner symbolises the story of the Chinese on the goldfields. It is a symbol of the myths surrounding the Chinese which provided the seeds for the political ideology and institutionalised racism which was behind the 1901 White Australia policy.

The banner represents the ever-present undercurrent of racism in Australian history.

10. The Lambing Flat Riot

On 30 June 1861, things exploded.

A large group of angry men, possibly over 1,000, armed themselves with pick handles and clubs. They marched through the area, attacking Chinese camps at Blackguard Gully and Back Creek.

The Chinese had heard the mob was coming and many fled. But that did not stop the violence. The mob destroyed everything — tents, tools, supplies. Some Chinese miners were beaten, robbed and even had their pigtails torn from their heads.

The attackers showed no mercy. They burned everything in sight, driving the Chinese from the area with nothing—no food, no tools, not even shelter.

11. The Aftermath

News of the riot shocked many people, but not everyone blamed the rioters. Some thought it was just the result of "too many Chinese" on the goldfields.

The name of the town was changed from Lambing Flat to Young, trying to distance it from its violent past.

Entrance to the Chinese Tribute Garden at Young

But history remembers what happened there.

Soon after, the NSW colonial government passed a law called the Chinese Immigration Regulation and Restriction Act in November 1861. This legislation made it harder for Chinese people to come to Australia and restricted where they could mine.

It was another one of the steps that led to the White Australia Policy.

12. What Can We Learn?

The stories of Buckland Valley and Lambing Flat remind us that Australia's gold rush was not just about adventure and riches. It was also a time when many people were treated unfairly because of their race or culture.

The Chinese miners came to Australia with hope, courage and determination. They brought skills, hard work, and traditions that helped shape our country.

Chinese Dragon Symbol

But they also faced terrible challenges — bullying, violence and laws designed to keep them out.

It's important for us to learn these stories so we can understand how racism affected people in the past — and how we must work to make things fairer today and in the future.

Panning for Gold

GLOSSARY

Alluvial gold — Gold found in riverbeds, usually easy to mine.

Credit-ticket system — A way of borrowing money to travel, then paying it back later.

Discrimination — Treating someone unfairly because of their race, gender, religion, etc.

Fraternal organisations — Groups formed to help support members, like clubs or societies.

Opium — drug that was smoked in the 1800s; some Chinese miners used it.

Riot — A violent disturbance caused by a group of people.

SOURCES

The author would like to acknowledge the following sources of information:

Aitchison, James (2019) "Non-fiction: madness and massacre: Chinese miners on the Victorian Goldfields" *Story Magazine in Arts & Culture*, Non-Fiction, January. https://storgy.com/2019/01/17/non-fiction-madness-and-massacre-chinese-miners-on-the-victorian-goldfields-by-james-aitchison/

Hill, Marji (2022) *Gold and the Chinese: Racism, Riots and Protest on the Australian Goldfields.* Broadbeach, Qld, The Prison Tree Press. (Gold! Hidden Stories of Australia's Past, Book 3)

Mo Yimei (1988) "Harvest of Endurance: a History of the Chinese in Australia 1788-1988" Sydney, Australia-China Friendship Society. http://www.multiculturalaustralia.edu.au/doc/yimei_1.pdf

National Museum of Australia. "Early Chinese Migrants". https://www.nma.gov.au/explore/features/harvest-of-endurance/scroll/early-chinese-migrants

ABOUT MARJI HILL

Marji Hill runs her art career alongside her career as an author. She is a highly respected international author as well as a seasoned business executive, researcher and coach.

Marji is passionate about promoting understanding between Australia's First Nations people and other Australians. The spirit of reconciliation was fostered in all her writings ever since she was a Research Fellow in Education at the Australian Institute of Aboriginal and Torres Strait Islander Studies (AIATSIS) in Canberra.

From 2008 to 2011, Marji was Deputy Chairperson of the Mosman Branch of Reconciliation Australia in Sydney. Following her Research Fellowship at AIATSIS in 1976 Marji, together with her late partner, Alex Barlow, produced more than seventy (70) books on all aspects of the First Nations people including the critical, annotated bibliography *Black Australia*.

In 1989 she was the Project Coordinator and one of the researchers and writers of *Australian Aboriginal Culture* the official Australian Government publication on First Nations people.

In 1988 *Six Australian Battlefields* was published by Angus and Robertson. A decade later it was re-published by Allen & Unwin as a paperback edition. Her nine-volume encyclopaedia, *Macmillan Encyclopaedia of Australia's Aboriginal Peoples* was published in 2000 and in 2009 she published *The Apology: Saying Sorry To The Stolen Generations*.

Marji's more recent publications extend to self-improvement and self-help with books like *Staying Young Growing Old* and *Inspired by Country* a self-help book about painting with gouache.

MORE BOOKS BY MARJI HILL

First Nations

Hill, Marji 2021 *Australian Aboriginal History: 5 Stories of Indigenous Heroes.* Broadbeach, Qld, The Prison Tree Press.

Hill, Marji 2021 *First People Then and Now: Introducing Indigenous Australians.* 2nd ed. Broadbeach, Qld, The Prison Tree Press.

Aboriginal Global Pioneers

Hill, Marji 2024 *Australian Aboriginal Origins: Earliest Beginnings.* Broadbeach, Qld, The Prison Tree Press. (Book 1)

Hill, Marji 2024 *Australian Aboriginal Trade: Sharing Goods and Services.* Broadbeach, Qld, The Prison Tree Press. (Book 2)

Hill, Marji 2024 *Australian Aboriginal Religion: Country and Dreaming.* Broadbeach, Qld, The Prison Tree Press. (Book 3)

Hill, Marji 2024 *Australian Aboriginal Fire: Managing Country.* Broadbeach, Qld, The Prison Tree Press. (Book 4)

Hill, Marji 2024 *Australian Aboriginal Medicine: Caring for People.* Broadbeach, Qld, The Prison Tree Press. (Book 5)

Self-improvement/Self-Help

Hill, Marji 2014 *Staying Young Growing Old.* Broadbeach, Qld, The Prison Tree Press.

Hill, Marji 2020 *How Big Is Your Why? An Author's Guide to Time Management and Productivity to Achieve Transformational Results.* Broadbeach, Qld, The Prison Tree Press.

Hill, Marji 2020 *A Create and Publish Toolbox: 101 Prompts In A Guided Journal To Help You Write, Self-publish, And Market Your Book on Amazon.* Broadbeach, Qld, The Prison Tree Press.

Hill, Marji 2021 *Inspired by Country: An Artist's Journey Back to Nature, Landscape Painting with Gouache.* Broadbeach, Qld, The Prison Tree Press.

Hill, Marji 2024 *Australian Paintings: Artworks by Marji Hill.* Broadbeach, Qld, The Prison Tree Press.

Gold

Hill, Marji 2022 *Gates of Gold: The Discovery of Gold, its Legacy and its Contribution to Australian Identity.* Broadbeach, Qld, The Prison Tree Press.

Hill, Marji 2022 *Shadows of Gold: Eureka and the Birth of Australian Democracy.* Broadbeach, Qld, The Prison Tree Press.

Hill, Marji 2022 *Gold and the Chinese: Racism, Riots and Protest on the Australian Goldfields.* Broadbeach, Qld, The Prison Tree Press.

Hill, Marji 2022 *Ghosts of Gold: The Life and Times of Jupiter Mosman.* Broadbeach, Qld, The Prison Tree Press.

Hill, Marji 2022 *Blood Gold: Native Police, Bushrangers & Law and Order on the Goldfields.* Broadbeach, Qld, The Prison Tree Press.

www.ingramcontent.com/pod-product-compliance
Lightning Source LLC
Chambersburg PA
CBHW041218240426
43661CB00012B/1082